BRITISH HISTORY

Tudors & Stuarts

1485-1714

KINGFISHER

KINGFISHER
Kingfisher Publications Plc
New Penderel House, 283–288 High Holborn
London WC1V 7HZ
www.kingfisherpub.com

Material in this edition previously published by Kingfisher Publications Plc
in *Children's Illustrated Encyclopedia of British History* in 1992

This revised, reformatted and updated edition published by
Kingfisher Publications Plc in 2002
1TR/0202/PROSP/RNB/140MA

2 4 6 8 10 9 7 5 3 1

A CIP catalogue record for this book is available from the British Library

ISBN 0 7534 0100 2

Printed in China

Editor: James Harrison,
with Jean Coppendale and Honor Head
Designer: Edward Kinsey
Proofreader: John Paton
Indexer: Yvonne Dixon
Cover design: Mike Davis

CONTENTS

THE TUDORS 1
Henry VII 2
Yorkist Threats 2
Lambert Simnel 2
Perkin Warbeck 3
Ireland Under Poynings 3
Henry VIII 4
The Renaissance 4
French and Scots Defeated 5
Henry, Divorce and the Church 5
Henry Closes the Monasteries 5
Union with Wales 6
Henry, King of Ireland 6
Henry's Failures in Marriage 7
The Reformation 8
Edward VI 8
Lady Jane Grey 8
Mary I 9
Elizabeth I 10
Good Queen Bess 11
Mary, Queen of Scots 11
Mary's Decline and Fall 11
Philip II Plans an Invasion 12
The Armada 12
Elizabeth's Court 12
Exploration 14
The Rise of the Naval Powers 14
Sir Francis Drake 15
Sir Walter Raleigh 15

THE STUARTS 17
James I 18
The Gunpowder Plot 18
Guy Fawkes 18
The Authorised Bible 18
The Puritans 19
Lady Arabella Stuart 19
The First Colonies 20
The Pilgrim Fathers 20
The Early Settlers 20
Charles I 22
Parliament's Petition of Right 23
King Against Parliament 23
The Civil War 24
Battles of the Civil War 25
The Commonwealth 26
Cromwell and Parliament 26
Cromwell: Lord Protector 26
Charles II 27
The Clarendon Code 27
The Great Plague 27
The Great Fire of London 28
Samuel Pepys's Diaries 28
The Dutch War 28
James II 29
James II and Catholic Plots 29
Whig and Tory 30
William and Mary 31
Irish Protestant Rule 31
Queen Anne 31
Blenheim Palace 31
Act of Union 32
Birth of Great Britain 32

Rulers of Britain 33
Glossary 33
Index 34

THE TUDORS
(1485 – 1603)

THE BEGINNING OF THE Tudor period in British history also signalled the end of the Middle Ages. The old feudal ways of life had largely disappeared and a new aristocracy drawn from the ranks of the growing middle classes was emerging. This was a period of great exploration and expansion in overseas trade, which gave the country a new source of wealth. The ideas of the Renaissance, which revived an interest in the art and learning of ancient Greece and Rome, marked the beginnings of modern culture and science. These ideas were spread by the use of the printing press. The Protestant Reformation, which began in Germany in an attempt to correct some of the worst features of the Roman Catholic Church, was adopted in England at first as a political move, and later as a matter of faith. The Tudors finally united Wales and England, so that one set of laws and rights applied to both countries. They also tried to complete the conquest of Ireland by settling English colonists in large estates there which were called plantations. Scotland suffered years of violent conflict.

Henry VIII with Jane Seymour and his three children; Mary *(far left)*, Edward *(left)* and Elizabeth *(far right)*.

Henry VII

Above: **Henry VII (1485-1509) was religious, hard-working and clever. He restored peace, justice and prosperity after years of conflict and civil war.**

THE LANCASTRIAN HENRY TUDOR defeated the Yorkist King Richard III at the battle of Bosworth Field in 1485, and became King Henry VII. This marked the end of the series of civil wars known as the Wars of the Roses which had been fought between two leading families called Lancaster (who had a red rose badge) and York (who wore a white rose badge).

Many nobles had been killed or their power weakened. Henry VII made sure this continued by getting rid of their private armies and by executing many for treason against the Crown. He then took over their estates. Henry also married a Yorkist princess to help bring the two families together.

YORKIST THREATS

Despite Henry VII's victory in the Wars of the Roses, he was still forced to watch constantly for threats to his throne from the few remaining Yorkist supporters. These supporters were often aided by foreign powers. France and Scotland in particular were traditional enemies of England. Richard III's younger sister, Margaret, the Duchess of Burgundy, twice found youths prepared to pretend to be claimants to the throne.

LAMBERT SIMNEL

The first pretender to the throne was Lambert Simnel, the son of an Oxford joiner. Yorkists tried to pass Simnel off as the missing Edward, Earl of Warwick, who had been imprisoned in 1485.

Below: **The Tudor succession. Lancastrian Henry VII consolidated the power of the Tudor dynasty by marrying Elizabeth of York.**

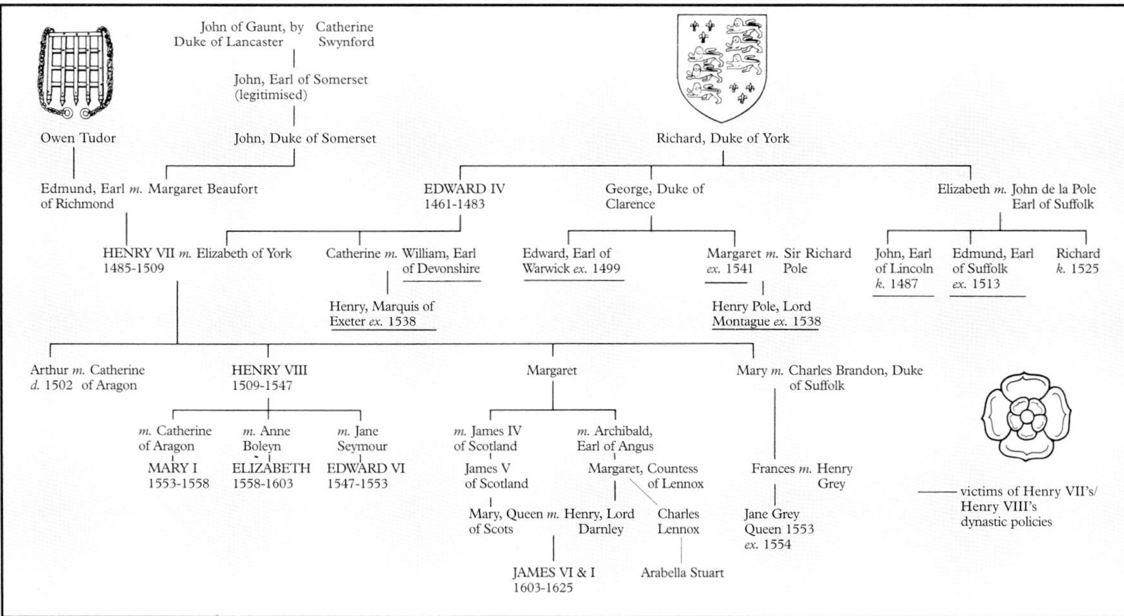

TIME CHART

- **1485** Henry Tudor defeats Richard III, becomes king (to 1509). Yeomen of the Guard founded. Edward, Earl of Warwick, son of Duke of Clarence, imprisoned
- **1486** Henry VII marries Elizabeth of York, daughter of Edward IV
- **1487** Lambert Simnel, pretending to be Earl of Warwick, proclaimed "King Edward VI" in Dublin. Simnel captured in England. Henry sets up special court of his council (later called Court of Star Chamber) to deal with offences the Common Law had proved unable to suppress
- **1488** Scottish rebels murder James III: son, James IV, becomes king
- **1489** First gold sovereigns minted
- **1491** Perkin Warbeck persuaded to impersonate Edward IV's son Richard of York
- **1492** Peace with France: Henry VII allows himself to be bought off. Warbeck finds support in Flanders
- **1494** Aberdeen University founded. Henry sends Sir Edward Poynings to Ireland to end Warbeck support. Statute of Drogheda (Poynings' Law) restates Henry's power
- **1495** Warbeck goes to Scotland: Sir William Stanley executed for supporting him
- **1496** James IV invades Northumberland in support of Warbeck. Anglo-Dutch treaty
- **1497** John Cabot discovers Newfoundland for Henry VII. Warbeck captured in Devon
- **1498** Warbeck imprisoned in the Tower of London
- **1499** Warbeck tried for treason and executed

The Irish, who had long been supporters of the Yorkist cause, rallied to Simnel. Lord Kildare, Lord Deputy of Ireland, had him crowned Edward VI in Dublin by the archbishop. Margaret of Burgundy supplied money and arms to support his cause and he sailed for England in 1487. However, Henry VII defeated him at Stoke in Nottinghamshire. Simnel was captured and made a servant in the royal kitchens where he lived for almost 40 years.

PERKIN WARBECK

The second claimant was Perkin Warbeck, son of a Flemish tax collector. Warbeck was supported in turn by the King of France, Duchess Margaret, the Holy Roman Emperor, and James IV of Scotland. He posed as Richard, Duke of York, who had been murdered with his brother Edward V in the Tower.

Warbeck claimed that he was spared when his brother was killed. Margaret supported him as her long lost nephew. He stayed with her in Flanders and eventually landed in England but was caught and hanged in 1499. Henry punished Flanders for harbouring Warbeck; he expelled all Flemings from England and moved England's wool market base from Antwerp to Calais. Another Yorkist claimant, Edmund de la Pole, known as the White Rose of England, was also supported by Margaret. He was executed in 1513.

IRELAND UNDER POYNINGS

To limit Irish support for Perkin Warbeck and the Yorkist cause, Henry VII sent Sir Edward Poynings to Ireland as Lord Deputy. Poynings called an Irish Parliament, which passed the Statute of Drogheda, also called Poynings's Law: no Irish Parliament could meet without the English king's consent, and no bill could be considered there without his permission. All bills placed before the Irish Parliament had to be passed by the English Privy Council beforehand. Also, all laws passed in England should also be the law in Ireland. This ended home rule in Ireland for centuries.

Below: **A royal judge hearing cases around England. Henry VII tightened his grip on government by restoring Henry II's system whereby royal judges travelled from town to town to administer the common law.**

- **1501** Arthur, heir to Henry VII, marries Catherine of Aragon. Palace of Holyrood House, Edinburgh, is begun
- **1502** Death of Prince Arthur
- **1503** Henry's daughter Margaret marries James IV, King of Scots. Arthur's brother, Henry, betrothed to his widow, Catherine
- **1504** First English shilling issued. Battle of Cnoc Tuagh: Lord Kildare, Lord Deputy of Ireland, defeats his rival Ulrich Burke
- **1507** Walter Chapman and Andrew Myllar set up first Scottish printing press
- **1509** Henry VII dies; succeeded by son Henry VIII. Henry marries Catherine of Aragon
- ***c.* 1509** English morality play *Everyman* first performed. Parliament grants Henry VIII customs revenue for life
- **1511** Henry joins the Holy League with Spain and the Pope against France
- **1512** Henry sends an unsuccessful expedition to capture Guienne in France
- **1513** Battle of Spurs: English defeat the French at Guingates (Thérouanne). Battle of Flodden: James IV of Scotland killed; James V, aged two, succeeds
- **1514** Henry's sister, Margaret, Queen Regent of Scotland, marries Archibald Douglas, Earl of Angus. Anglo-French truce: Henry's sister Mary marries Louis XII. Thomas Wolsey becomes Archbishop of York
- **1515** Duke of Albany becomes Protector of James V: Margaret flees to England. Wolsey becomes Chancellor. Work starts on Hampton Court
- **1517** May Day riots: London apprentices attack foreign traders. Albany goes to France, and is not allowed to return home

Henry VIII

Above: **Henry VIII (1509-1547) had been a great supporter of the Roman Catholic Church, but his divorce from Catherine of Aragon caused a break with the Pope which led to the Reformation of the English Church.**

HENRY VIII BECAME KING IN 1509 at the age of 17. A short time before that he was betrothed to Catherine of Aragon, youngest daughter of the Spanish rulers Ferdinand and Isabella. She had been married to Arthur, Henry's elder brother, to strengthen an alliance between England and Spain. But Arthur died suddenly, so Henry VII decided his younger son should marry Catherine because he was worried that he may have to return her dowry. The marriage was at first forbidden by the Church because the couple were too closely related, but Henry VII persuaded the Pope to allow it.

THE RENAISSANCE

The Renaissance is the modern name for the revival and spread of learning that took place from the 1400s onwards. It began in Italy, and spread throughout Europe. The works of ancient Greek and Roman writers and philosophers were widely read. Artists developed new styles of painting, including the use of perspective, or the illusion of distance. The speed with which these new ideas spread was due to the use of printing presses which began at this time. The Renaissance came to England in the reign of Henry VII, who invited Italian scholars and artists to his court. It found its greatest expression in literature: the Tudor period was a time of great poetry. It was also a time of major musical activity, especially the composition of Italian-style madrigals for groups of singers.

Left: **Henry VIII loved entertainments. At one banquet he provided "24 great beeves, 100 fat muttons, 91 pigs and 14 dozen swans". He played several musical instruments, enjoyed dancing and composed songs; it has been claimed that he wrote the famous song *Greensleeves*. Henry was well educated and he enjoyed discussing religion, art and other Renaissance subjects.**

- **1517** Martin Luther publishes his 95 Theses in Germany, starting a movement later known as the Reformation
- **1518** Wolsey is made papal legate. Peace of London between France and England. Royal College of Physicians founded
- **1519** Henry VII's chapel at Westminster Abbey completed
- **1520** Field of Cloth of Gold: Henry meets Francis I of France. Holy Roman Emperor Charles V visits Henry: Treaty of Calais
- **1521** Diet of Worms: Luther condemned as a heretic. Pope Leo X gives Henry title of Defender of the Faith. Albany returns to Scotland
- **1523** Thomas More becomes Speaker of the House of Commons
- **1525** Peace between England and France. William Tyndale translates New Testament into English
- **1526** Peace between England and Scotland
- **1527** Henry asks the Pope to end his marriage to Catherine of Aragon
- **1529** Wolsey stripped of power. Thomas More becomes Lord Chancellor
- **1530** Death of Wolsey
- **1531** Clan Donald and the Macleans rebel: pacified by James V. Clergy agree to acknowledge Henry as their "protector and only supreme head"
- **1532** More resigns as Lord Chancellor
- **1533** Henry marries Anne Boleyn. Act of Restraint of Appeals forbids appeals to Rome. Thomas Cranmer now Archbishop of Canterbury; declares Henry's marriage with Catherine void; Pope excommunicates Henry

Above: **Henry VIII met the French king in 1520 at the Field of Cloth of Gold – so called because of the luxurious display, by both kings, of pavilions and tents made and furnished with satins, velvets and cloths of gold.**

- **1534** Act of Supremacy: Henry VIII makes himself Head of the Church in England
- **1535** Thomas More executed on a charge of treason. Thomas Cromwell made Vicar-General. Miles Coverdale makes first translation of Bible into English
- **1536** Catherine of Aragon dies. Anne Boleyn executed; Henry marries Jane Seymour. Small monasteries dissolved. Pilgrimage of Grace: northern revolt against religious changes. Act of Union unites Wales with England
- **1537** Jane Seymour gives birth to a son, Edward: she dies
- **1538** James V of Scotland marries Mary of Guise
- **1539** Henry orders the dissolution of larger monasteries
- **1540** Henry VIII marries Anne of Cleves, but soon divorces her and marries Catherine Howard. Thomas Cromwell executed for treason. War with France

FRENCH AND SCOTS DEFEATED

In 1511 Pope Julius II asked Henry VIII, the King of Spain and the Holy Roman Emperor to help him drive the French out of Italy. Henry agreed, hoping to reconquer some of England's former territories in France. His first expedition failed, but in 1513 he led a second expedition and at Guingates (Thérouanne) he won a short battle known as the Battle of Spurs after the speed at which the French fled. In that year the Scots invaded England to aid France. At Flodden Field, in Northumberland, the Scots faced an English army half its size but led by an experienced general, Thomas Howard, Earl of Surrey. English cannon, arrows and tactics won the day. The Scots lost King James IV and 10,000 men.

HENRY, DIVORCE AND THE CHURCH

After 18 years of marriage to Catherine of Aragon, Henry VIII had no male heir, only a daughter, Mary, born in 1516. No queen had ever ruled all England, and the Wars of the Roses showed the damage that could be caused by disputes over the succession to the throne. In 1527 Henry decided to divorce Catherine, who was unlikely to bear more children, and find a wife who could give him a son and so secure the Tudor dynasty.

Henry ordered Cardinal Wolsey to ask the Pope to grant a divorce. The Pope refused, and Wolsey fell from power. So that Henry could grant himself a divorce, he decided to separate the Church in England from the authority of the Pope, a move carried out by a series of Acts of Parliament. Meanwhile Henry had married a lady of the court, Anne Boleyn. In 1533 the new Archbishop of Canterbury, Thomas Cranmer, declared Henry's marriage with Catherine invalid (using the original argument that he could not marry his brother's widow) and his marriage with Anne legal. Anne soon produced a child, but it was another girl, Elizabeth. Once again Henry was disappointed, and, not having a son, he turned against Anne.

In 1536 a charge of adultery was brought against Anne. She was accused of treason, tried and beheaded. Henry then married Jane Seymour, who produced the longed-for son which they named Edward.

HENRY CLOSES THE MONASTERIES

English monasteries were in decline in the 1500s, and many of them were badly run. Henry's first attack against them came from Wolsey, who obtained papal permission to suppress 40 of the smaller monasteries.

- **1541** Henry VIII takes the title of King of Ireland. Wales gets representation in the English Parliament
- **1542** Catherine Howard executed. England and Scotland at war. Scots lose battle of Solway Moss. James V of Scotland dies; daughter Mary succeeds
- **1543** Henry marries Catherine Parr
- **1544** English army invades Scotland, occupies Edinburgh. Boulogne captured
- **1545** Scots win battle of Ancram Moor. The *Mary Rose*, refitted in 1536, sinks in the Solent
- **1546** Peace with France. Cardinal Beaton, a Scottish statesman, assassinated
- **1547** Henry VIII dies; succeeded by Edward VI, aged nine; Duke of Somerset appointed Protector
- **1548** Heresy laws abolished in England

Above: **The administrative regions of Wales after the Act of Union in 1536. Wales was now completely absorbed into the English system of government.**

In 1536 Henry ordered nearly 400 of the remaining small ones to be dissolved, and took over their land and property. The rest of the smaller monasteries were then dissolved and the monks pensioned off.

This move was so beneficial to Henry's finances that in 1539 Henry decided to dissolve the larger monasteries. Monasteries that resisted were destroyed and their monks brutally killed. Henry gained still more wealth by selling off the monastery lands to rich nobles, but the charity and care which the monks had given to the poor and needy was a great loss.

UNION WITH WALES

In 1536 Henry VIII decided that Wales should be united with England. By the Act of Union it became part of England. An Act in 1541 gave Wales the right to send members to the English Parliament in Winchester. The Welsh shires were created by the Tudors, and English law was extended to Wales, with English as the official language of the law courts.

HENRY, KING OF IRELAND

Having made himself Supreme Head of the Church in England, Henry VIII decided to extend his powers to Ireland, where the English owned large estates including most of Leinster and Meath.

Right: **In 1536 Henry closed all the smaller monasteries and confiscated their property to help his finances. In 1539 all the larger monasteries were closed. In just ten years Henry VIII closed all of England's 800 monasteries.**

Right: **Hans Holbein the Younger's painting of Sir Thomas More (third on the left) and his family. More, once Henry's friend and Lord Chancellor, was to accept the King as supreme authority over the Church. He was later canonized by the Catholic Church.**

In 1541, an Irish Parliament was called in Dublin and gave Henry the title of King of Ireland. More than 40 Irish chiefs and Anglo-Irish nobles surrendered their lands to the King and received them back as vassals, the same terms by which English barons held their lands. Henry tried but failed to force Protestantism on Catholic Ireland.

HENRY'S FAILURES IN MARRIAGE

After Jane Seymour's death, Henry's chief minister, Thomas Cromwell, arranged a marriage with a German princess, Anne of Cleves. The marriage was to ally England with the Protestant princes of northern Germany – an alliance on which Cromwell was very keen. Henry had never met Anne, but as part of the marriage arrangements he received a portrait of her. One story has it that when Anne arrived she was so plain that the disappointed Henry described her as "the Flanders mare". However, there is no reason to believe the painting falsely flattered her face.

The marriage was soon dissolved, and Henry married Catherine Howard, a beautiful young noblewoman. Catherine was unfaithful to him, and Henry had her beheaded.

Henry's last marriage was to a widow, Catherine Parr, who knew how to manage him, and who outlived him. Henry died in 1547. He left behind a son, Edward VI, who was a sickly child of only 10 years of age, and two unmarried daughters, Mary and Elizabeth. This meant that the succession to the throne was far from secure.

FOCUS ON THE MARY ROSE

The *Mary Rose* was Henry VIII's greatest warship. It could carry 200 crew, 185 soldiers and 30 gunners. There were some 140 cannon and hand guns. But it capsized and sank before Henry's eyes a few kilometres from Portsmouth Harbour during an engagement with a French invasion fleet on July 19, 1545.

The wreck was located in about 12 metres of water in 1971 by Alexander McKee and raised in 1982 with the current Prince of Wales in attendance. Among the artefacts recovered were cannons, longbows, gold coins and sail maker's and barber-surgeon's tools. The remains are now housed in Portsmouth alongside HMS *Victory* in an exciting display of Britain's maritime history.

THE REFORMATION

Although Henry VIII had broken ties with the Pope, he still supported the beliefs and customs of the Roman Catholic faith. During the reign of his son Edward VI, England was to move steadily away from Catholicism and towards the Protestant religion, in the movement later known throughout Europe as the Reformation. The Reformation had started in Germany in 1517 when Martin Luther protested against certain elaborate practices of the Roman Catholic Church. Forty years later, half of Europe was Protestant.

EDWARD VI

Edward was only nine when he came to the throne, and the government was in the hands of his uncle, Edward, Duke of Somerset, who had the title Protector. Somerset abolished the laws against heresy, removed images and altars from the churches, and introduced an English-language *Book of Common Prayer*, which was compiled by Thomas Cranmer. By an Act of Uniformity in 1549, the use of this Prayer Book was made compulsory. In another change, priests who had previously had to live as single men were now allowed to marry.

LADY JANE GREY

In 1550 the Duke of Northumberland took over from Somerset as Protector and persuaded Edward to name Lady Jane Grey as his heir to the throne. Lady Jane, the grand-daughter of Henry VII, was married to Northumberland's son Guildford Dudley. Edward agreed to Lady Jane Grey becoming his successor because he feared that the Crown would otherwise pass to his sister, Mary, who was a devout Catholic and who would make England a Catholic country again.

Edward died in 1553 but his death was kept secret and Lady Jane was proclaimed queen. But less than two weeks later Mary's claim to the throne was recognized and Lady Jane and her husband were imprisoned.

Above: **Edward VI (1547-1553) was reserved, courteous, intelligent, and intellectual. But he became seriously ill and died, probably of consumption, aged only 15 years of age.**

- **1549** First Prayer Book in English; made compulsory by Act of Uniformity. Clergy allowed to marry. Fall of Duke of Somerset (executed in 1552), succeeded by Duke of Northumberland as Protector. Images and altars in churches ordered to be destroyed
- **1553** Edward VI dies; Lady Jane Grey proclaimed queen. After nine days, Jane deposed: Mary Tudor becomes queen. Duke of Northumberland executed. Sir Thomas Wyatt leads rebellion. Sir Hugh Willoughby and Richard Chancellor's voyage in search of a northwest sea passage to Asia
- **1554** Wyatt, Lady Jane and her husband Guildford Dudley executed. Mary I marries Philip II of Spain
- **1555** Catholic Restoration begins. Bishops Latimer and Ridley among Protestants burned

At first Mary refused to execute Lady Jane Grey, Dudley and Northumberland, for attempting to secure a Protestant succession. But a rising in their favour led by Sir Thomas Wyatt made Mary realize they would always be a danger to her while they lived. They were beheaded in the Tower of London on February 12, 1554.

MARY I

Mary I came to the throne in 1553. She had been unhappy ever since Henry VIII had divorced her mother, Catherine of Aragon. Her greatest wish now was to undo the Reformation and restore England to the Roman Catholic faith. Mary's husband, the devoutly Catholic Philip II of Spain, encouraged her plans. Opposition to the Church of Rome was strong and could only be crushed by harsh measures. Mary began by stopping all clergy from reading the *Book of Common Prayer*. In Mary's five-year reign 275 Protestants were put to death for refusing to convert back to Catholicism.

Right: **Mary I (1553-1558) was strong-willed, a shrewd politician and believed passionately that it was her duty to return England to the Catholic Church.**

Above: A chained English Bible in a church. During the Reformation the use of the English Bible and the *Book of Common Prayer* was made compulsory by the Act of Uniformity of 1549. It was also forbidden to remove these books from churches so they were chained up to keep them safe.

Left: The coronation procession of Edward VI in 1547 as it moved down Cheapside from the Tower of London (visible to the left) to Westminster Abbey (to the right). London south of the Thames had hardly been developed, but both Henry VII and Henry VIII had spent lavishly on royal residences in London.

- **1555** John Knox returns from exile to Scotland
- **1556** Archbishop Cranmer burned at the stake. Cardinal Pole, papal legate, becomes Archbishop of Canterbury. Earl of Sussex becomes Lord Deputy of Ireland
- **1557-59** War with France
- **1558** French recapture Calais. Mary, Queen of Scots, marries dauphin Francis of France. Mary I dies; succeeded by sister Elizabeth I (to 1603). Acts of Supremacy and Uniformity re-enacted
- **1559** Dauphin Francis becomes Francis II of France: Mary, Queen of Scots assumes title Queen of France
- **1560** Church of Scotland established. Mary of Guise (wife of James V and mother of Mary Stuart) deposed as Scottish regent. Reformation imposed in Ireland
- **1561** Mary returns to Scotland after husband's death

Left: The burning in Mary's reign of two leading Protestant bishops, Latimer and Ridley, in 1555. Archbishop Cranmer, who was himself later burned at the stake, is shown praying to God to give them strength. At the final moments Ridley said to Latimer: "We shall light such a candle as shall never be put out".

Among the victims were nobles and clergy such as Archbishop Cranmer. Mary has since acquired the nickname "Bloody Mary".

Mary died broken-hearted in 1558. Her husband did not love her and lived abroad and she had no child or heir. The loss of Calais – England's last foothold in France – in 1558 was the final blow for this unhappy queen. "When I die," Mary said, "Calais will be written on my heart."

Elizabeth I

HENRY VIII'S YOUNGER DAUGHTER, Elizabeth, ascended the throne in 1558, with no opposition. She restored the Protestant religion and gradually established the Church of England.

Elizabeth I was a remarkable woman. She spoke five languages besides English: Greek, Latin, French, Italian and Spanish. She was a talented musician, a graceful dancer and a fine archer. She was also a very skilled politician, calculating and extremely clever. Elizabeth said of herself that she had "the body of a weak and feeble woman, but the heart and stomach of a king, and a king of England too".

FOCUS ON THE GREAT TUDOR PALACES

There are many fine Tudor manors, houses and palaces all over England – from the black-and-white half-timbered houses of Chester, to the Great Houses of Hardwick Hall, and especially Hampton Court Palace (*below*). Five wives of Henry VIII lived in the splendid Hampton Court situated beside the Thames, and it is said to be haunted by the ghost of Catherine Howard, Henry's fifth wife. The palace was offered to Henry in 1526 by Cardinal Wolsey who wanted to keep in favour with the king. Tournaments were held in the Tiltyard Gardens, and the Clock Court, Great Hall and Gate House are all of Tudor origin. Bess Hardwick, one of the richest people in Elizabeth I's reign, was actively involved in the designs of her great house, Hardwick Hall, Derbyshire in 1597. Now that the barons' wars were over, these palaces were built without castle-style fortifications.

Above: **This portrait was painted when Elizabeth was 56 years old, just after England's victory over the Spanish Armada in 1588.**

GOOD QUEEN BESS

Elizabeth's reign lasted for 45 years. She remained unmarried and independently powerful, and dominated her male advisors. She died without an heir. Her court celebrated her as Gloriana, and the ordinary people referred to her as Good Queen Bess. Her enemies were mostly Roman Catholics, who were badly treated and often went in fear of their lives. Her reign also witnessed the execution of Mary Stuart and the dramatic attack of the Spanish Armada.

MARY, QUEEN OF SCOTS

Mary Stuart became Queen of Scotland when she was just a week old on the death of her father, James V. She was brought up as a Catholic in France, and was married at the age of 16 to the dauphin of France. When he became king in 1559, she became Queen of France as well as of Scotland. Through her descent from Henry VIII's sister, Margaret, Mary was also Elizabeth's heir and so she had a claim to the English throne too.

Mary was celebrated as the most beautiful woman of her time, an accomplished and graceful child of the French court. She was also a clever politician – almost as dominating as Elizabeth of England.

MARY'S DECLINE AND FALL

In 1561 Mary's husband died and she returned to Scotland. The Scots were mainly Protestants and disapproved of Mary's religion and of her foreign ways. She next married her cousin, Henry Stuart, Lord Darnley, who was a jealous man. Darnley helped murder Mary's secretary, David Rizzio, suspecting him of being the queen's lover.

Mary, in turn, was determined on revenge. Soon after their son James was born, Darnley was strangled and the house where he was staying blown up. Suspicion fell on James Hepburn, Earl of Bothwell, and increased when Mary married him. The Scottish lords did not like Bothwell. Scottish opposition to Mary forced her to give

Right: **The execution of Mary Stuart, in February 1587. Elizabeth had kept her prisoner for 18 years. Finally she became too great a threat as a focus for Catholic plots to be allowed to live.**

Left: **The sinking of a great Spanish galleon by English ships in 1588. The Spanish Armada was beaten by the skill of the English fleet and violent storms.**

up the throne in favour of her baby son, James VI. Mary fled to England, throwing herself on Elizabeth's mercy. But Elizabeth made her a prisoner. Mary was considered a ringleader in a series of Catholic plots against Elizabeth.

Mary was charged with involvement in the Babington Plot and was tried and found guilty. Elizabeth eventually allowed Mary's execution.

PHILIP II PLANS AN INVASION

Under Elizabeth I, England became Protestant again. Philip II of Spain was determined to dethrone her. He wanted to restore England to the Catholic faith that his wife Mary I had so rigorously tried to reinstate. Elizabeth had angered Philip by supporting the Dutch in their war of independence against Spain. British seamen, were also raiding Spanish colonies and plundering treasure ships. Philip planned an invasion.

THE ARMADA

In 1588 an Armada, or fleet, of 130 Spanish warships set sail up the English Channel, to pick up soldiers from Dunkirk in France and land them on the English coast. The English prepared an emergency fleet led by experienced sailors Lord Howard of Effingham, Francis Drake, John Hawkins, and Martin Frobisher. The English fought a running naval battle with the Spanish in the Channel. Eventually the Armada took shelter in Calais harbour, but Drake sent in fireships. To escape the danger of their whole fleet catching fire, the Spaniards hurriedly raised anchor and sailed out to another confused battle. Both sides had run short of cannon fire, and with no further supplies available, the Armada was forced by bad weather to escape into the North Sea.

The Armada returned home after sailing round the British Isles. It lost 44 ships out of 130. Many surviving ships had to be scrapped. This did not end the conflict between Spain and England which continued because Elizabeth could not bear to hold peace talks with Spain. It was left to her successor, James I, to make peace in 1604.

ELIZABETH'S COURT

The court around Queen Elizabeth glittered like the queen herself. Hers was an age when, it seemed, every gentleman aspired to be a poet or a musician, or both. For example, Sir Philip Sidney, the brave soldier who died fighting the Spanish at Zutphen, in the Netherlands, was a fine poet.

Left: **Rich Elizabethan men wore embroidered jackets, fur-lined robes, and short padded trousers called breeches. Noble women wore wide skirts stiffened by hoops and padding and lace ruffs around the neck.**

Elizabeth's reign saw a flourishing of plays and poetry. The Globe Theatre, since restored in 1996, could hold nearly 3,000 people.

The outstanding playwright was William Shakespeare, but at the time he was one of many highly regarded dramatic poets. Others had more than one occupation. Playwright Christopher Marlowe, murdered in a tavern brawl, is thought to have been a secret agent; Edmund Spenser, who wrote *The Faerie Queene*, helped in the plantation (settlement) of Ireland.

England led the way in the writing of music for keyboard instruments, and much traditional church music was written at this time. Two outstanding musicians were Thomas Tallis and his pupil William Byrd.

Towards the end of Elizabeth's reign madrigals (love poems sung by several voices without musical accompaniment) were introduced into England. Thomas Morley edited a collection of madrigals in honour of Elizabeth, called *The Triumphs of Oriana*, but it was not published until after the Queen's death.

Above: Sir Philip Sidney, Elizabethan poet, courtier, diplomat and soldier, was idolized by the English people. He has been called the "jewel of Elizabeth's court".

FOCUS ON THE THEATRE

England's first theatre was built at Shoreditch. It was based on the enclosed courtyard of big inns, where actors used to perform. The theatre was built by actor-manager James Burbage. The building was simply called 'The Theatre'. It was open to the sky, like the later Globe Theatre where Shakespeare acted. Other theatres, such as the Blackfriars and the Whitefriars, had roofs.

- **1562-64** Elizabeth I sends forces to France to help the Huguenot (French Protestants) in their revolt against the Catholic government. John Hawkins becomes the first English slave trader
- **1565** Mary, Queen of Scots marries her cousin Lord Darnley. Royal Exchange, London, founded. John Hawkins brings back sweet potatoes and tobacco
- **1566** Darnley and others murder David Rizzio, Mary's secretary
- **1567** Darnley murdered; Mary marries Bothwell. Mary abdicates; succeeded by son James VI, aged one. Earl of Moray becomes Regent: Mary held prisoner
- **1568** Mary escapes to England and becomes prisoner of Elizabeth
- **1569** Rebellion in north of England: Durham Cathedral plundered
- **1570** Pope Pius V declares Elizabeth a usurper and heretic
- **1572** Duke of Norfolk and Earl of Northumberland executed for treason. Francis Drake attacks Spanish harbours in the Americas
- **1573** John Hawkins begins to reform the Navy
- **1575** MP Peter Wentworth claims freedom from arrest for Members of Parliament for discussing key areas of government
- **1576** James Burbage opens first theatre at Shoreditch
- **1577-80** Drake's voyage round the world. Drake returns from voyage and is knighted by Elizabeth
- **1583** Sir Humphrey Gilbert claims Newfoundland for England. Edinburgh University founded

Exploration

WHEN THE ITALIAN EXPLORER Christopher Columbus approached Henry VII in 1492 for funds to pay for his voyages of discovery, Henry, known for his financial caution, turned him down. Columbus was eventually funded by King Ferdinand and Queen Isabella of Spain, who benefited greatly from his discoveries in America.

Five years later Henry VII did finance John Cabot's expedition. Cabot was a sailor from Genoa, Italy, who was based in Bristol. His voyage led eventually to the founding of the first British colony in America, at Newfoundland (in present-day Canada). Later a rich cod-fishing trade developed there. Henry VII was pleased with the results and gave Cabot a pension of £20.

THE RISE OF THE NAVAL POWERS

From the end of the 15th century, Portugal, Spain, France, the Netherlands, and later England, started on a series of daring expeditions to claim new lands and wealth on the other side of the world.

The European powers intended to ship spices, precious metals, cotton and other materials back home. To do this they all needed strong navies. Henry VIII helped to establish a reliable English navy of 50 to 70 ships and about 8,000 sailors, as well as a network of dockyards. One of the new ships he had built was the *Mary Rose*, named after his favourite sister, but it capsized and sank before his eyes on July 19, 1545.

Above: **A galleon sets sail. A team of sailors unfurl the mainsail. Galleons were very large ocean-going ships, four times as long as they were wide. They had a special deck for cannons. They replaced earlier ships called carracks, which were broader, slower and less manoeuvrable.**

- **1584** Sir Walter Raleigh tries to establish a colony near Roanoake Island, Virginia (now North Carolina)
- **1586** Drake raids Santo Domingo and Cartagena in West Indies. Francis Walsingham uncovers Babington Plot, involving Mary, Queen of Scots. Mary condemned for treason
- **1587** Mary, Queen of Scots, executed. Drake partly destroys Spanish fleet at Cadiz. War with Spain breaks out
- **1588** Philip II launches "Invincible Armada" against England, but it is destroyed
- **1590** First Shakespeare plays performed
- **1592** Plague kills 15,000 Londoners
- **1593** Poet and playwright Christopher Marlowe murdered
- **1595** Hugh O'Neill, Earl of Tyrone, heads rebellion in Ireland
- **1595** Spaniards land in Cornwall, burn Mousehole and Penzance. Raleigh explores Orinoco River in South America

Left: **Elizabeth I knights Walter Raleigh in 1584. In the same year Raleigh sent ships to North America to explore the east coast.**

SIR FRANCIS DRAKE

Sir Francis Drake was an accomplished explorer and sea captain who served Elizabeth loyally and helped England become a major sea power. Between 1577 to 1580, he and his men on the *Golden Hind* made an epic voyage around the world, the first crew to do so. Elizabeth and others bought shares in the voyage, the object of which was to plunder the Spanish colonies as well as to explore a way by sea to Asia and its riches. Elizabeth gave Drake a knighthood on his return.

SIR WALTER RALEIGH

Walter Raleigh was a great soldier, explorer, and writer. The story of Raleigh removing his coat and placing it over a large puddle so Elizabeth could avoid getting wet may not be true. But he did become one of the Queen's favourites at Court. Elizabeth wanted colonies for England – chiefly to establish trading posts for merchants and so bring wealth to the country.

In 1584, Raleigh sent 100 colonists across the Atlantic to America to find gold and take possession of new lands. Queen Elizabeth was impressed with the venture and so he named the new land Virginia after her, because people called her the "Virgin Queen". Raleigh was also the first person to introduce tobacco and potatoes into England from the American colonies.

Compass

Astrolabe

Backstaff

Above: **The most important navigation instrument used in the 1500s was the compass, which showed in which direction the ship was travelling. The astrolabe and the backstaff used the sun to measure the distance north or south of the equator.**

- **1597** John Harington describes his new invention, the water-closet
- **1598** Battle of the Yellow Ford: Irish defeat the English
- **1599** Earl of Essex becomes Lord Deputy of Ireland; he concludes truce with Tyrone, but is arrested at home. Lord Mountjoy succeeds Essex as Lord Deputy of Ireland. East India Company founded
- **1601** Essex dabbles in plots, is tried for treason and executed. Spanish army lands in Ireland, but surrenders at Kinsale
- **1603** Mountjoy crushes Irish rebellion. Elizabeth I dies; succeeded by James I of England (James VI of Scotland). Amnesty in Ireland. Main and Bye Plots against James I: Raleigh is jailed for involvement

Below: A cutaway view of a two-decker galleon. **1** gundeck; **2** anchor cable; **3** cookhouse; **4** hold; **5** rudder; **6** captain's table.

Below: Produce bought back from the Americas by Elizabethan explorers included potatoes and tobacco leaves.

Charles II (1660-1685) had to flee to France when Civil War broke out, but returned on Cromwell's death.

THE STUARTS
(1603 – 1714)

ELIZABETH I'S HEIR WAS JAMES VI of Scotland, son of Mary Stuart, Queen of Scots. The family of Stuart had ruled Scotland for 232 years before James VI united England and Scotland under a common crown, though not yet in law. Eventful as those years had been, they were not so dramatic as the following 111 years during which the Stuarts ruled over England, Wales, Scotland and, in name, over Ireland. In that time the combined nation underwent two revolutions: the English Civil War 1642-1645 which ended with the execution of Charles I, and the Glorious Revolution of 1688. This was a bloodless affair, when the Dutch prince William of Orange was invited to become King of England in place of Catholic James II, and so secure the Protestant succession for the English throne.

At first the Stuart monarchs claimed to rule by divine right; eventually it was made plain that they ruled by the consent and invitation of Parliament. The death of Charles I brought a period known as the Commonwealth when England was ruled by Oliver Cromwell and Parliament. On Cromwell's death, Parliament called Charles II back from exile and in 1660 the monarchy was restored. By the end of the Stuart period England and Scotland were formally united, and Ireland was more controlled by the English than before.

Meanwhile, the British were expanding overseas. Many colonies, were set up in North America. The religious tensions at home drove some people abroad to escape persecution. The most famous group was the Pilgrim Fathers, who founded the Plymouth Colony in America in 1620. Elsewhere, British traders established settlements in southern Africa and India which would eventually develop into an empire.

James 1

THE NEW KING James I of England was, as he said himself, an "old and experienced king". He had already ruled Scotland for 25 years as James VI. The son of Mary Stuart and Lord Darnley, he believed in the divine, or God-given, right of kings to rule, and had managed the Scottish Parliament more or less as he liked. The English Parliament was far less easy to handle, insisting that the king could rule only by its consent. James supported the Protestant Church and was determined to enforce its practices.

Above: **James I (1603-1625) is said to have suffered from a stammer and dribbled. But he was an intelligent king who wrote against the evils of tobacco and introduced a new English translation of the Bible.**

THE GUNPOWDER PLOT

James I enforced an old law against Roman Catholics which stated that they had to go to Protestant churches, or be fined. A group of Catholics decided to start a revolution by blowing up the Houses of Parliament at a time when James was to be there. But one of the conspirators warned a relative, who was likely to be endangered by the plot: "Retire yourself into the country... they shall receive a terrible blow this Parliament, and yet they shall not see who hurts them." The relative passed the information on to the authorities who searched the cellars of Parliament.

GUY FAWKES

Guy Fawkes, one of the conspirators, was caught red-handed guarding several barrels of gunpowder. The leader of the conspiracy was not, in fact, Fawkes but Robert Catesby. Fawkes endured hours of torture on the rack, but refused to incriminate anyone else. Fawkes and the other conspirators confessed under torture and were tried for treason and executed.

AUTHORISED BIBLE

When James I came to the throne there were five English translations of the Bible in use. He ordered a new translation. Fifty churchmen and scholars completed the task in seven years. The result was the Authorised Version, or King James Bible – which is still the most popular English version after more than 350 years. The beauty of its language has been a lasting influence on all English-speaking peoples. It also provided a major inspiration for the Puritan movement which later overthrew Charles I.

Left: **Guy Fawkes (*third from right*) with his fellow plotters. They stacked firewood and gunpowder under the Houses of Parliament, and planned to set fire to them when James I opened Parliament on November 5, 1605.**

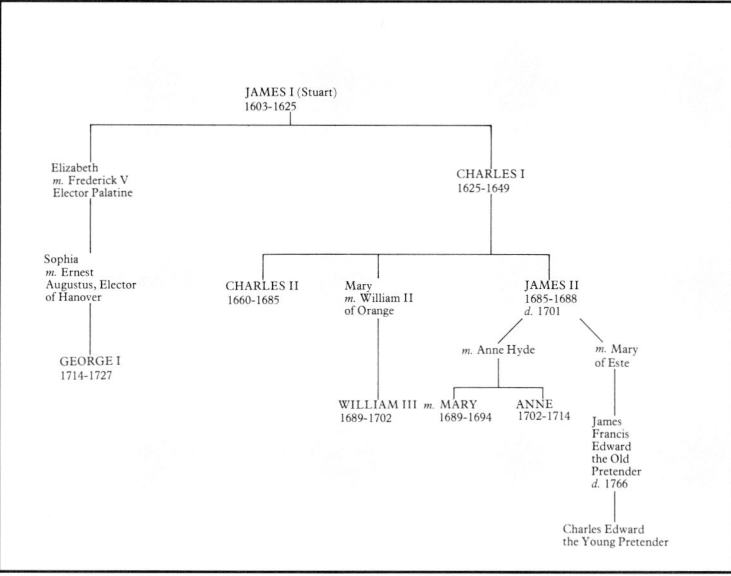

Left: **The Stuart family tree. By 1603 James I's family name of Stewart was being spelled Stuart – the French way. This arose because James's grandfather had taken French nationality in 1537. James was a Protestant but he accepted Catholics and was prepared to allow his heir, Charles, to be engaged to the French Catholic princess, Henrietta Maria.**

THE PURITANS

The Reformation of England had brought very few changes to the Church and many Catholic practices continued. The Church of England retained bishops, ceremony and vestments. But many people wanted a simpler, purer form of worship, with no bishops or elaborate religious ritual. They became known as Puritans. Some Puritans left England for America, where they could worship as they chose. But most remained determined to fight oppression rather than evade it. They were the dominant influence in Parliament in its later clash with Charles I.

Below: **The title page of the Authorised Version, or King James Bible, showing its publication date: ANNO DOM. 1611. The Bible remains the most widely read book ever published in the English language.**

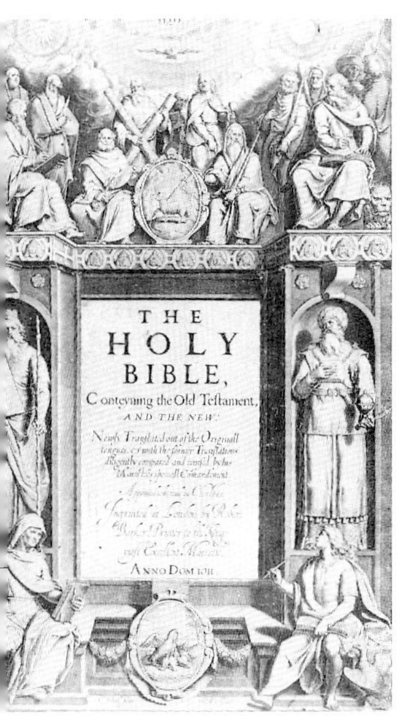

LADY ARABELLA STUART

Lady Arabella Stuart was James's first cousin, and had a claim to the throne on Elizabeth's death. For this reason Elizabeth I and then James, were determined that she should marry only someone they could trust.

Arabella fell in love with William Seymour, later Duke of Somerset. He was a great-great-grandson of Henry VII and, in Henry VIII's will, had been made the next heir to the British throne after Elizabeth. James forbade this match, but the couple married secretly in 1610. A conspiracy against James I was hatched, but the couple were found out and imprisoned. Arabella and Seymour planned an escape, Seymour got away, but Arabella was recaptured and confined in the Tower, where she died, insane. Seymour later became a leading Royalist general in the Civil War.

- **1603** James VI of Scotland becomes James I of England
- **1604** James enforces Act of Uniformity. James's first Parliament rejects his plan to unite England and Scotland, but James proclaims himself King of Great Britain, France and Ireland. Peace with Spain
- **1605** Gunpowder Plot: Guy Fawkes caught. Act of Uniformity proclaimed in Ireland
- **1606** Guy Fawkes and other plotters are executed for treason. James raises customs duties without consent of Parliament
- **1607** First permanent settlement in America at Jamestown, Virginia
- **1609** Plantations (settlements) plan for Irish lands from confiscated Irish estates to be granted to settlers from mainland Britain
- **1610** James's cousin Lady Arabella Stewart marries William Seymour: the couple are imprisoned
- **1611** James dissolves Parliament. Authorised Version of the Bible is published
- **1615** Lady Arabella Stuart dies. English fleet defeats Dutch fleet off Bombay
- **1616** Willem Schouten rounds Cape Horn. Walter Raleigh released from Tower. Navigator William Baffin searches for Northwest Passage to Pacific Ocean and discovers Baffin Bay
- **1617** Raleigh attacks Spanish colonies
- **1618** Thirty Years War starts
- **1618** Raleigh executed for treason
- **1619** Dutch ships bring first negro slaves to the colony of Virginia

The First Colonies

THE BEGINNINGS OF the British empire took place in Elizabethan times with Sir Walter Raleigh's unsuccessful attempt to set up a colony at Roanoke in North America. But James I distrusted Raleigh and finally had him executed. In 1607 three ships sailed into present-day Chesapeake Bay in Maryland where they built a fort at Jamestown (named after James I). Of the 104 colonists, almost half died that summer from malaria, typhoid and shortage of food. It was here that the Algonquin princess Pocahontas befriended Captain John Smith and saved him from being clubbed to death. She later came to London and attended the royal court. She died in 1617 on her way back to Jamestown. The colony itself eventually prospered and plantations of tobacco were established with the help of the local native American tribes. Later the colonists brought in black slaves from West Africa to work the fields.

THE PILGRIM FATHERS

On December 15, 1620 a very different colony was established farther north by just over 100 English Puritan farmers and craftsmen. These colonists became known as the Pilgrim Fathers. They were seeking a place where they could worship without persecution. They left Plymouth in a ship called the *Mayflower* and dropped anchor off Cape Cod in Massachusetts.

The colony flourished when native American farmers taught the settlers how to grow corn (maize). In the autumn of 1621 they held their first harvest supper. They feasted on geese, turkeys, duck, shellfish, watercress and wine and invited the native Americans to the first Thanksgiving Day. That day, towards the end of November, is now a national holiday in the United States. Families and neighbours meet together to share the traditional Thanksgiving meal of turkey, cranberry sauce and pumpkin pie.

THE EARLY SETTLERS

The first settlers' houses were built of wood, of which there was plenty in the surrounding forests. The roofs were made of thatch and later of thin sheets of hardwood called shingle. The first chimneys were made of stone and later of brick. The colonists' life was hard: they spun thread, wove cloth, and tanned leather for jackets and shoes, and made candles from fat or beeswax. Although there was plenty of land to grow crops and they were free from religious persecution life was tough for these first settlers so that even after ten years, their colony still numbered only about 300 people.

Left: **The Hudson Bay Company was started in 1670 especially to trade in furs. Here fur trappers trade with native Americans in northern Canada in the 1700s.**

Above: In 1636, Roger Williams established a permanent settlement at Providence, Rhode Island (the smallest state in the United States). Williams was a Puritan minister who was driven out of Massachusetts because he accused the Puritans of not being tolerant enough. Williams bought the land from two native American Narragansett chiefs. Setting up a new colony held many dangers – land had to be cleared, even in the harsh winter, and supplies were scarce. However, by 1643 there were four settlements in Rhode Island which united in 1663.

Left: The *Mayflower* took 102 Puritan colonists and 47 crew safely across the Atlantic. The ship was only about 30 metres long and 6 metres wide. The height of the space below deck was only one metre (high enough for a small child) and there were no portholes. Here the men, women and children rolled about and were sick as the ship was tossed around by the ocean swell for two months. The only water available for washing was sea water. Nevertheless, only one colonist and four crew died on the epic voyage.

- **1620** Pilgrim Fathers sail from Plymouth to colonize America. They arrive at Cape Cod and found the Plymouth Colony
- **1621** James I calls third Parliament: it votes money for English involvement in Thirty Years War. Great Protestation asserts the rights of Parliament; petition against Catholicism
- **1623** George Villiers, James's favourite, becomes Duke of Buckingham. Charles and Duke of Buckingham fail to negotiate Spanish marriage. First English settlement in New Hampshire
- **1624** James calls fourth Parliament. Marriage arranged between Charles and Henrietta Maria of France
- **1625** James dies: succeeded by Charles I. Charles marries Henrietta Maria. Parliament votes customs' duties for king for one year only
- **1626** Charles summons second Parliament which impeaches Buckingham and is dissolved. War with France. Charles collects taxes without Parliament's approval
- **1628** Charles calls his third Parliament: MPs present Petition of Right, and oppose king's collection of taxes

Charles I

Below: **Charles I shown from three different angles by the Dutch portrait painter, Van Dyck, in 1635. Charles's reign was to end with the English Civil War of 1642-1646. The Parliamentary army, led by Oliver Cromwell, defeated the King's forces at Naseby and Charles was imprisoned. But when he was discovered plotting another campaign, he was tried and beheaded in 1649. The Bible he was given before his execution can be seen at Chastleton Hall in Oxfordshire.**

ON JAMES I's DEATH IN 1625, his son Charles I inherited a difficult financial situation. Parliament believed that "the King should live of his own", meaning that money from taxes and Crown lands should pay all government expenses, and also the expenses of the Court.

It was usual for Parliament to vote a new sovereign money for life in the form of customs duties. However, James I had found expenses rising faster than income. This was partly due to inflation, caused by the arrival of gold and silver from the Americas. James resorted to a variety of methods to raise money, including creating the title of baronet and selling it to wealthy candidates.

Irritated at Charles's attempts to ignore them, Members of Parliament voted taxes to Charles for one year only. Charles had a constant struggle to find money by other means to finance himself. Finally he raised taxes without Parliament's consent, but this led to a bitter conflict with those wanting to protect the rights of Parliament.

- **1628** Charles I adjourns Parliament. Physician William Harvey publishes discovery of blood circulation
- **1629** Parliament reassembles to condemn Charles's actions: Commons bar door to King's officers. Charles dissolves Parliament and rules without it
- **1630** John Winthrop leads 1,000 Puritan settlers to Massachusetts, in America, and founds Boston
- **1631** English mathematician William Oughtred introduces multiplication symbol x
- **1632** Lord Baltimore receives charter for Maryland colony in America
- **1633** William Laud appointed Archbishop of Canterbury. Sir Thomas Wentworth becomes Lord Deputy in Ireland
- **1634** Wentworth calls Irish Parliament, imposes the 39 Articles on Ireland
- **1635** Charles raises Ship Money (an old tax, dating back to the Danish invasion) from inland towns
- **1636** Charles rules that the Scottish Church should be governed by bishops
- **1637** John Hampden tried and found guilty for refusing to pay Ship Money
- **1638** National Covenant in Scotland challenges King's power
- **1640** Short Parliament refuses funds requested by Charles, who dissolves it. Scots win victory: Charles agrees to truce and pays £850 a day to the Scots to stop further military advances. Long Parliament (to 1653). Strafford and Laud impeached
- **1641** Court of Star Chamber and High Commission abolished. MPs set out grievances in Grand Remonstrance. Strafford executed

Above: **An ornate English chair of the period. Chairs in the later 1600s were upholstered for the first time, with rich fabrics for greater luxury. Furniture of the period was also elaborately carved, and had very ornamental designs.**

Above: **A fashionable lady and gentleman during the reign of Charles I. Lace, braid, muslin and embroidery were used to decorate clothes, and colourful plumes were worn in hats.**

PARLIAMENT'S PETITION OF RIGHT

In the first four years of his reign Charles I called three Parliaments and disagreed with all of them. At the root of the problem were money and war: first against Spain, and then against France to support the Huguenots (the French Protestants). Parliament was all for the war, and voted funds for it – but at a price.

That price was embodied in the Petition of Right, presented to the king by the House of Commons in 1628. It demanded an end to: martial law; billeting of troops on people; imprisonment without trial; and forced loans and taxes (raised without the consent of Parliament). The king was forced to accept the petition.

KING AGAINST PARLIAMENT

The quarrel between the king and Parliament continued, because Charles refused to stop collecting his own taxes after the time limit set by Parliament. The Commons passed three resolutions condemning the actions of Charles and his ministers. When the Speaker of the House, Sir John Finch, tried to announce that the king had dismissed Parliament, the Members of Parliament held him in his chair while the resolutions were put to the vote, and the doors were barred against Black Rod, the royal messenger from the House of Lords. Today, the Commons slam their door in Black Rod's face whenever he comes to summon them to hear the Queen's Speech in the Lords at the opening of Parliament.

After this incident Charles did dissolve Parliament, and he ruled for 11 years without it. Like his father James I, Charles firmly believed in the doctrine of the divine right of kings, and rejected the role of Parliament to run the country.

The Civil War

THE ENGLISH CIVIL WAR OF 1642 to 1646, or Great Rebellion as some people called it, was sparked off by religion. Charles tried to impose bishops on the Scottish Church, and the Presbyterians refused to accept them. They signed a Covenant to resist, and raised an army. Charles made peace, but it did not last. He had to summon Parliament to obtain money to pay for his army, but dissolved it after just three weeks. Then the Scots invaded England, and Charles persuaded them to halt on payment of £850 a day. Desperate, he had to call Parliament again in 1640.

This Parliament began by impeaching Strafford and Laud, the king's hated ministers, for treason, and later had Strafford executed. They abolished two ancient courts – Star Chamber and High Commission – which Charles had used to raise money illegally. John Hampden and John Pym led Members of the Commons to insist on reforms. Charles tried to arrest them and three other Members for treason. He failed, and soon armed conflict broke out.

The opposing sides were the Parliamentarians, or Roundheads (they had their hair cut short), and the Royalists, or Cavaliers – because they wore long hair like the knights (*chevaliers* in French) of old.

Above: **The first major battle of the Civil War took place at Edgehill in 1642; the last took place at Worcester in 1651. Key battle sites: king raises his standard at Nottingham 1642; Edgehill 1642; Marston Moor 1644; Naseby 1645; surrender of Royalist headquarters at Oxford 1646; Preston 1648; Dunbar, 1650; Worcester, 1651.**
● Royalist headquarters
■ Parliament's headquarters

- **1642** Charles I tries to impeach five members of the Commons. Civil War begins (to 1646). Drawn battle of Edgehill
- **1643** Alliance between Scots and Parliament.
- **1644** Battle of Marston Moor: Oliver Cromwell defeats Royalists. Second battle of Newbury: Royalist victory
- **1645** Laud executed. Self-Denying Ordinance discharges MPs from civil and military office. Battle of Naseby: final defeat of Charles, who surrenders to the Scots.
- **1646** Surrender of Royalist headquarters at Oxford
- **1647** Scots surrender Charles to Parliament. Army, in conflict with Parliament, seizes Charles
- **1648** Scots try to help Charles: defeated by Cromwell at Preston
- **1649** Charles tried for treason and executed

Left: **In the English Civil War, it was Oliver Cromwell and his New Model Army of plainly dressed Roundheads who finally beat the king's splendidly clad Cavaliers.**

BATTLES OF THE CIVIL WAR

The king's main support was in the west; Parliament held the east, and London. The actual fighting took place in a relatively small part of the country. But the impact of the Civil War was felt everywhere, not least because family loyalties were split. Early battles were inconclusive: the king's forces had better cavalry under the command of his nephew Prince Rupert (who had fought in Europe in the Thirty Years War). But the Parliamentary army, with its musketeers and pikemen, proved steadfast on the whole against the cavalry attacks. They were also later trained to charge and proved so steady in attack that Rupert called these well-trained forces Ironsides. Led by Oliver Cromwell, the Ironsides defeated Rupert and the Royalist army at Marston Moor in 1644 and won all the north of England.

Parliament was so impressed it reorganized its forces into a New Model Army, based on Cromwell's Ironsides. This army grew to 20,000 men and was strictly disciplined, properly equipped, and regularly paid. It was led by General Fairfax with Cromwell as second-in-command. It defeated the king at the battle of Naseby in 1645, the last major battle of the Civil War. Charles escaped to Scotland but was handed over to Parliament by the Scots. Eventually, Parliament came to the conclusion that it could not trust the king and Charles became the only British monarch to be tried for treason and executed.

Above: Even though Charles I had been defeated on the battlefield he still believed he should not give up any of his power. He tried to start another campaign by forming an alliance with Scotland and this led to his being tried for treason in 1649. It was Cromwell who pushed for Charles to be tried in a court of law.

Above: Charles I's son and heir, Prince Charles, fought against Cromwell in the Civil War. Trying to flee to France, he was nearly caught by Cromwell's soldiers at Boscobel in Shropshire, but hid in an oak tree until they had passed.

Left: Before the executioner's axe at Whitehall Palace on January 30, 1649 Charles I behaved with great courage. He wore an extra shirt in case anyone thought he shivered for fear rather than cold. His body was secretly buried in Windsor Castle.

The Commonwealth

THE EXECUTION OF Charles I left England firmly in the hands of Parliament and its army. For the next 11 years the country did not have a king. This period was called the Commonwealth.

Cromwell had to defend the Commonwealth against Dutch, French and Spanish support for the young Charles II, as well as Scottish and Irish rebellions. Charles II was proclaimed king in Scotland, and the Irish also rallied to the Royalist cause. Cromwell took an army to Ireland, where he subdued the Royalists with great severity. Charles and an army of Scots marched into England, where they were defeated by Cromwell at Worcester. Charles escaped to France.

Above: **During the Commonwealth many people wore plainer clothes with no trimmings or frills. Colours were often black, dark brown and grey. Women wore linen caps. Men and women wore grey or green woollen stockings and square-toed shoes.**

Above: **Charles II (1660-1685) was known as the Merry Monarch. His return marked the revival of entertainments discouraged by the Puritans. Theatres reopened, and hunting and gambling increased.**

CROMWELL AND PARLIAMENT

The country was governed by the so-called Rump Parliament, made up of those Members of the Commons remaining when Cromwell and the army had forced through Charles I's trial and execution. It was this Parliament that had declared the Commonwealth and also abolished the House of Lords. Members of the Rump were mostly Puritans.

Oliver Cromwell, however, was the real power in the land. He turned the Rump out, and called a new Parliament, nominated by the Army and the independent Nonconformist Churches. It was nicknamed Barebone's Parliament, after one of its more extreme religious Members, Praise-God Barebone. This Parliament also failed to provide a strong government.

Above: **Oliver Cromwell was born in 1599. He studied law in London and sat in Parliament, where he opposed the king. He was a dedicated, religious man with a strong personality.**

CROMWELL: LORD PROTECTOR

From 1653 Oliver Cromwell ruled as Lord Protector. He was offered the Crown by Parliament but refused to be King Oliver. As Protector, Cromwell made the country peaceful and also made it stronger abroad. He allowed some religious freedom, except for Catholics in Ireland. He put down the Levellers who believed in the abolition of distinctions of rank. Cromwell still tried to rule in partnership with Parliament, but they could not agree and so instead Cromwell used his army to enforce what he thought was right. To maintain his army he had to increase taxes which made him very unpopular. Cromwell died, probably of cancer, in 1658.

- **1649** Commonwealth set up with Cromwell in charge. Irish rise in favour of Charles II
- **1650** Charles II crowned in Scotland
- **1651** Cromwell defeats Charles at Worcester: Charles escapes to France
- **1652-54** War with Dutch over shipping
- **1653** Cromwell turns out the Rump Parliament, calls a nominated Parliament. Cromwell becomes Lord Protector
- **1655** Cromwell dissolves Parliament: rule of the Major-Generals. Anglican services banned
- **1656-59** War with Spain: England captures Dunkirk from Spaniards
- **1656** Cromwell excludes opponents from second Parliament
- **1657** Cromwell refuses Crown
- **1658** Cromwell dissolves Parliament. Death of Cromwell: succeeded by son Richard

Charles II

CROMWELL WAS GIVEN a king's funeral. At this time no one was sure who should replace him – though most people wanted to return to having a monarchy. Before he died, Oliver Cromwell nominated his son to succeed him. Richard Cromwell was a weak and mild man and the Army, still the main power in the land, turned him out. Amid all the chaos, General George Monk, commander in Scotland, organized new elections, and a fresh Parliament recalled Charles II from exile to be king in 1660. Charles travelled from Holland with 100 ships, and timed his entry into London to coincide with his birthday. He was received with great popular acclaim.

THE CLARENDON CODE

After the upheavals and trauma of the Civil War and Commonwealth, people feared the Puritans both on religious grounds and also as a threat to the monarchy. Parliament therefore passed a group of Acts, which were known as the Clarendon Code, named after the king's chief minister, the Earl of Clarendon.

The Code compelled all clergymen and people holding office in local and national government to take Communion in accordance with the rites of the Anglican Church. People who did not attend Church of England services would be punished. Nonconformist prayer-meetings were limited to five people, and their clergy were barred from coming nearer than eight kilometres to a town.

Charles II is thought to have had some Catholic sympathies, but he knew that to keep his Crown he had to support the Church of England. So he went along with Parliament's rigid laws against Catholics and Puritans alike. Only on his deathbed did he convert to the Roman Catholic faith.

THE GREAT PLAGUE

The London that Charles II returned to in 1660 was the largest city in Europe with 500,000 inhabitants (Paris had 350,000). However, health and hygiene in the city had not improved since the time of the Black Death in the Middle Ages. The streets were just as dirty and full of disease and rats were everywhere. Many houses were built closely together and streets were very narrow. This meant that any epidemic would spread rapidly.

FOCUS ON THE GREAT PLAGUE

On June 7, 1665, Samuel Pepys noted in his famous diary that "this day, much against my will I did in Drury Lane see two or three houses marked with a red cross upon the doors". This was the tell-tale sign that the occupants had become sick with the plague. The Great Plague, from 1664 to 1665, was an outbreak of bubonic plague in the southeast of England which killed 68,596 people – almost 20 percent of London's population. There was no cure: bodies would be carried out at night in carts to special mass pits. Drivers rang handbells and called out "Bring out your dead!" They were paid well for a dangerous job. Pepys provides a gritty day-to-day account of the plague in his diaries.

- **1659** New Parliament called; quarrels with the Army and is dissolved. Rump Parliament returns, persuades Richard Cromwell to resign
- **1660** George Monk, commander in Scotland, marches to London. Monk rules as captain-general. Long Parliament recalled. Charles II promises amnesty. Army disbanded. Act of Indemnity
- **1661** Charles calls his first Parliament
- **1662** Charles marries the Portuguese princess Catherine of Braganza; sells Dunkirk to France
- **1664** British take New Amsterdam (now known as New York) from the Dutch. Royal Marines formed
- **1665** War between England and the Netherlands (to 1667). Great Plague in London

Right: **The Great Fire of London in 1666 destroyed the medieval city and made 100,000 people homeless. The diarist Samuel Pepys gives a harrowing report of London in flames: "All over the Thames, with one's face in the wind, you were almost burned with a shower of fire drops."**

THE GREAT FIRE OF LONDON

The following year saw another disaster, the Great Fire of London. This began in a baker's house in Pudding Lane and quickly swept through the crowded wooden houses. It raged for several days, until houses were blown up to make gaps which the fire could not cross. King Charles himself directed the firefighters and even worked among them. The fire was not an unmixed disaster; filthy alleys were burned down, the plague was halted, and London was rebuilt with wider streets and improved water supplies.

After the fire, many new buildings were erected in stone and brick, instead of wood. Among them were 52 churches designed by the architect. Christopher Wren, including his most well-known building, St Paul's Cathedral, built in 1675-1710.

SAMUEL PEPYS'S DIARIES

We know a lot about both disasters in London thanks to the diaries of Samuel Pepys. He was a civil servant helping to improve the navy. He also had access to Charles II's Court and was a great gossip. He kept a diary for nine years but wrote it in secret and in code. The diaries were then lost, and not rediscovered until 1825. The diary has since became one of the most famous ever written in Britain. Its pages bring alive the London of Charles II with its theatres, coffee houses, horse-racing, gambling and beautiful women.

THE DUTCH WAR

The English and Dutch were rivals in fishing and trade, and when the Dutch started settlements on the Hudson River of North America among the English colonies, the merchants appealed to

Left: **A sea battle fought between heavily armed galleons during the Dutch War of 1665-1667. Some ships carried more than one hundred guns. Here a Dutch ship has had its masts and sails blasted away by a barrage of English cannon fire. However, it was the Dutch who sailed up the River Medway in Kent, and captured the royal flagship *Royal Charles*.**

Above: **James II (1685-1689) was the first Catholic monarch after Mary I. Arrogant, obstinate and a fervently religious, James failed to re-establish a Catholic dynasty. His reign ended in flight and exile.**

Parliament and war was declared. It began with an English victory in a naval battle of 300 ships off Lowestoft in 1665. In 1667, when the English fleet was unable to put to sea because of lack of supplies, the Dutch sailed up the Medway, raided the naval dockyard at Chatham, and captured the flagship *Royal Charles*, which they took back to Holland as a war trophy.

Other battles were fought during the two years that the war dragged on. One, in June 1666, in the North Sea, lasted for four days. The Dutch were led by their great admiral De Ruyter, and the English fought under George Monk, Duke of Albemarle. Both sides claimed victory.

James II

CHARLES II HAD NO CHILDREN with his wife Catherine of Braganza from Portugal, but he had many mistresses who gave him 14 illegitimate sons and daughters. The most popular of his sons was James, Duke of Monmouth, called the Protestant Duke. Monmouth was a capable soldier, who had commanded English troops during the Dutch War. When Charles II died, his brother James became king in 1685, Monmouth thought he could rally the Protestant cause against the Catholic James and win the throne for himself. But he picked his time badly: James had not been king long enough to make himself unpopular, and the motley army Monmouth was able to raise was defeated at the battle of Sedgemoor, in Somerset. Monmouth was executed for treason, and so were nearly 300 of his followers. A further 800 were sold as slaves to Barbados.

JAMES II AND CATHOLIC PLOTS

James's succession was also threatened by fears of a Catholic plot. The Exclusion movement, led by the Whigs – the first political party in English history – believed the new king would try to restore the Roman Catholic religion. They wanted to exclude him from the throne. From 1688 James tried to introduce pro-Catholic measures including a Declaration of Indulgence which cancelled all laws against Nonconformists (chiefly Catholics). Seven bishops were arrested because they would not read out the Declaration in church, but were found not guilty. The arrests were very unpopular.

- **1666** French declare war on England. English privateers take Tobago in the West Indies. Great Fire of London started from Pudding Lane: 180 hectares of the city destroyed
- **1667** Dutch burn the English fleet in the River Medway. Peace of Breda between Dutch, French and English
- **1668** Charles II's brother James, Duke of York, becomes a Roman Catholic
- **1670** First British settlement in South Carolina, America. Secret Treaty of Dover between Charles II and Louis XIV of France. Hudson's Bay Company formed to trade in Canada
- **1672** England goes to war against the Dutch
- **1673** Test Act excludes Catholics and Nonconformists from holding public office
- **1674** Peace declared with the Dutch. Ex-pirate Henry Morgan becomes Governor of Jamaica
- **1675** Greenwich Observatory founded. Work begins on St Paul's Cathedral, London
- **1677** William of Orange marries Mary, daughter of James II
- **1678** John Bunyan publishes the first part of *Pilgrim's Progress*
- **1679** Disabling Act bars any Roman Catholics from entering Parliament
- **1680** William Dockwra sets up penny post in London
- **1681** Charles grants the right to settle Pennsylvania, America, to Quaker William Penn. Parliament meets in Oxford, but is dissolved
- **1685** Charles dies; succeeded by his brother James II. Monmouth lands to claim the throne: defeated at Sedgemoor. The Bloody Assize: hundreds of rebels hanged or sold as slaves

- **1686** James II introduces pro-Catholic measures
- **1689** Son born to James. Seven English lords invite William of Orange to England. William lands at Torbay: James flees. Convention Parliament elected: declares James to have abdicated, offers throne to William III and Mary II jointly. Window tax (to 1851)
- **1690** William defeats James at the battle of the Boyne in Ireland: James flees to France
- **1692** Massacre of Glencoe, Scotland
- **1694** Bank of England founded. Death of Mary II
- **1697** Treaty of Ryswick ends French war
- **1701** Act of Settlement establishes Protestant succession. James II dies: France recognizes his son as James III (the Old Pretender). War of the Spanish Succession begins
- **1702** William III dies; succeeded by sister-in-law Anne. First English daily newspaper, the *Daily Courant* published
- **1703** Work begins on Buckingham Palace, London
- **1704** English capture Gibraltar from Spain as a naval base. English win battle of Blenheim
- **1707** Union of England and Scotland as Great Britain
- **1708** Robert Walpole becomes Parliamentary Secretary for War
- **1710** St Paul's Cathedral finished. Duke of Marlborough falls from favour
- **1711** South Sea Company formed
- **1713** Treaty of Utrecht ends War of the Spanish Succession
- **1714** Death of Queen Anne

Left: William of Orange landing in Britain on November 5, 1688. He led a powerful fleet as a precaution but met with no resistance. William's peaceful invasion is known as the "Glorious Revolution," and Parliament willingly offered William and Mary the Crown. They reigned for 14 years.

Above: William and Mary (1689-1702) ruled as joint monarchs. They were both Protestants and during their reign a number of Acts were passed which limited royal power. The Protestant succession was also secured by the Act of Settlement of 1701 which barred Catholics from the British throne and also prevented any British monarch from marrying a Catholic.

WHIG AND TORY

The terms Whig and Tory came into use at this time as terms of abuse for political opponents. Whig was originally a name for Scottish cattle thieves, but it was applied to those people who wanted to exclude James II from the throne because of his Catholic sympathies. James made a promise to uphold the Church of England (despite being a Catholic) to quieten the protesters. Tory was originally the name given to Irishmen whose land had been taken away and who had become outlaws. But the term Tory was given to those people who supported James II and the claims of the Crown. How the terms came to be applied to English political groups is obscure. But the name became thoroughly established in British politics.

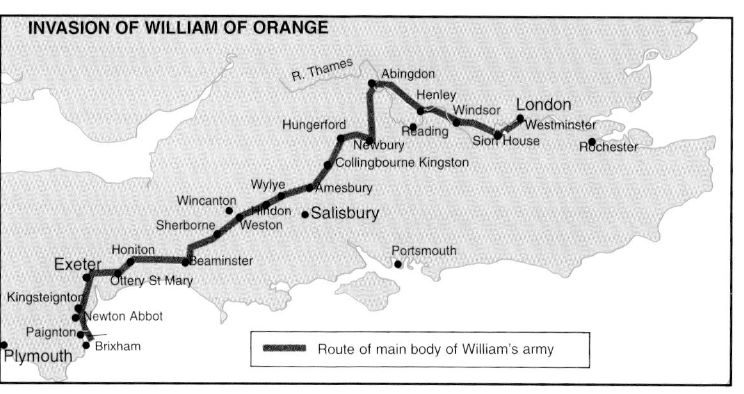

Left: By the time William of Orange reached London, James II had fled the country to seek more support across the Channel in France.

William and Mary

JAMES II'S OBVIOUS ATTEMPTS to favour Catholics so angered the Protestants that Parliament invited the Dutch Protestant prince, William of Orange to come and deliver the country from its unpopular ruler. Parliament was prompted to this action by the birth of a son to James by his second wife. This pushed the claim of the Protestant Princess Mary, James's daughter and William's wife, into second place.

William's invasion consisted of some 250 ships which anchored at Torbay in Devon in November 1688. William with his Protestant army landed to press his wife's claim to the throne. Mary had refused to accept the Crown unless Parliament also offered it to her husband. When William arrived in London James fled to France. As a result Parliament agreed that James had vacated his throne and offered the Crown to William and Mary.

IRISH PROTESTANT RULE

After he was deposed by William of Orange, Irish Catholics sided with James, while the Protestants of Ulster supported William. James went to Ireland where he raised an army. In 1689 he laid siege to Londonderry where thousands of Irish Protestants sought refuge. He failed to take the city and William finally defeated James at the battle of the Boyne in 1690. This battle is still celebrated annually by the Protestant Orangemen of Ulster. James fled back to France, where he died in 1701.

Left: **Anne (1702-1714) was a shy, plain woman. She had 17 children, all of whom died in infancy or childhood. During her reign science, art and literature flourished.**

QUEEN ANNE

The Treaty of Ryswick made in 1697 between England, France, Holland and Spain had acknowledged William III as the rightful King of England, and Anne, James II's Protestant daughter, as his successor. She became Queen Anne I in 1702, aged 37, and was the last Stuart monarch. Her life was full of great personal sadness and bad health. She had 17 children but all of them died in infancy or childhood. Her reign was dominated by the War of the Spanish Succession abroad and by rivalry between Whigs and Tories at home.

By the terms of the Act of Succession of 1701 the throne was to pass to the nearest Protestant heir, in the House of Hanover. Anne hated her German cousins and refused to allow them to come to England. But as her reign drew to an end she sent an envoy to the future George I, assuring him of her friendship. By so doing she played a vital role in ensuring that there was a peaceful change of dynasty.

Right: **This tapestry at Blenheim Palace shows John Churchill, Duke of Marlborough at the battle of Blenheim in 1704 where he crushed Louis XIV's army. Other notable English victories in the War of the Spanish Succession included Ramillies (1706), Oudenarde (1708), and Malplaquet (1709). After his victory at Blenheim the magnificent Blenheim Palace was built near Woodstock in Oxfordshire. It was based on designs by the architect Sir John Vanbrugh and the gardens were landscaped by Capability Brown.**

ACT OF UNION

The political union of England and Scotland, which James I had tried to bring about when he became King of England in 1603, was finally accomplished in 1707. The Scots did not accept the English Act of Settlement, which in 1701 had settled the Crown on the descendants of the Protestant Sophia of Hanover (grand-daughter of James I and mother of the future George I). There was an unspoken threat that Scotland might, when Queen Anne died, bring back the Catholic Stuarts by making James II's son, James Francis Edward the Old Pretender, King of Scotland.

This threat brought the English Parliament to support the move towards union. The Scots had come to realize that their country could no longer prosper as an independent nation. Under the Act of Union, their Parliament gained free trade with England, and cash to pay off huge debts acquired in a disastrous colonising venture in Darien in Central America. The Scots also kept their own legal system and Presbyterian church.

BIRTH OF GREAT BRITAIN

The resulting kingdom of England and Scotland was called Great Britain. For some years after the union the people of Scotland, felt they were at a disadvantage in an unequal partnership. The English majority in the combined Parliament meant that measures which favoured England at Scotland's expense were passed. One example was a special tax on linen, which was unimportant in the south but a major industry north of the border. However, the union was in Scotland's favour as it was now able to trade with England's various colonies. After decades of conflict the two countries combined in an uneasy but peaceful alliance.

Right: **The Act of Union was passed in 1707, legally uniting the kingdoms of England and Scotland. The English flag, the red cross of St George on white *(top left)*, and the white cross of St Andrew of Scotland on a blue background *(top right)*, were joined to form the first Union flag, soon called the Union Jack. The diagonal red cross of Ireland's St Patrick was added in 1801.**

FOCUS ON THE COFFEE HOUSES

During the 1600s coffee was brought to England from the Middle East. In 1652 the first coffee house was opened in London. Coffee houses quickly spread to become popular places where people went to gossip, do business deals and discuss politics. In 1688 Edward Lloyd opened a coffee house in Tower Street, a rendezvous for people who would insure ships and their cargoes, and read a publication called *Lloyd's News*, which gave important shipping details. From this original 17th-century coffee house sprang the modern Lloyds, the world's foremost shipping insurers. From about 1704 single news-sheets – the first form of newspapers – could also be bought and read at coffee houses.

RULERS OF BRITAIN

HOUSE	NAME	REIGN	MARRIED	CHILDREN
TUDOR	Henry VII	1485 – 1509	Elizabeth of York	Arthur, Henry VIII, Margaret, Mary
	Henry VIII	1509 – 1547	1. Catherine of Aragon	Mary I
			2. Anne Boleyn	Elizabeth I
			3. Jane Seymour	Edward VI
			4. Anne of Cleves	
			5. Catherine Howard	
			6. Catherine Parr	
	Edward VI	1547 – 1553		
	Mary	1553 – 1558	Philip II of Spain	
	Elizabeth I	1558 – 1603		
STUART	James I	1603 – 1625	Anne of Denmark	Henry, Charles I, Elizabeth
	Charles I	1625 – 1649	Henrietta Maria of France	Charles II, James II, Mary
	Commonwealth	1649 – 1653		
	Protectorate	1653 – 1660		
	Charles II	1660 – 1685	Catherine of Braganza	
	James II	1685 – 1689	1. Anne Hyde	Mary (marries William of Orange), Anne
			2. Mary of Modena	James Francis Edward (Old Pretender)
	William and Mary	1689 – 1702		
	Anne	1702 – 1714	Prince George of Denmark	

GLOSSARY

Anglican belonging to the Church of England, with its doctrine and rituals

blockade closing up of a place or country, by military or naval forces, generally to starve it into obedience or surrender

canonize to formally declare a person a saint. Used by the Roman Catholic Church

Catholics supporters and followers of the Church of Rome

colony settlement by people in new territory still subject to their country of origin

Covenanters Scottish Presbyterians who resisted Charles I's and Charles II's attempts to introduce bishops and Anglican church rituals

dissolution act of breaking up the monasteries; also dismissal of Parliament with a view to summoning a new one as and when the monarch required it

divine right the belief that monarchs received their authority directly from God and so were not answerable to Parliament

dowry money and other assets a rich woman was expected to bring with her when marrying

East India Company Trading company given monopoly of eastern trade by Elizabeth I in 1600. Later in conflict with Dutch East India Company

excommunicate to exclude someone from communion, privileges and public prayers of the Church

Holy Roman Empire a federation of European states and princes that lasted from 800 to 1803

impeach to accuse a public official of a crime against the state, such as treason, and the legal process of removing them from office

monopoly sole possession or control of trade in something

Non-Conformists those (as well as catholics) who did not agree with the established Church of England. Also called dissenters

Parliament highest body in Britain responsible for making laws, consisting of the House of Commons, the House of Lords and the sovereign

Privy Council a group of people appointed for life by the sovereign to be his or her private advisers

Protestantism religion of any branch of the western Church separated from the Roman Catholic Church

Reformation religious and political movement of the 16th century to reform the Roman Catholic Church, which resulted in Protestantism

regent ruler of a country during the absence, minority or incapacity of the monarch

Renaissance revival of interest in art and learning of ancient Greece and Rome, from about 1400 to about 1600

ship money a tax to raise money to build ships, revived illegally by Charles I

statute a law or rule made by a body or institution, meant to be permanent and expressed in a formal document; especially, an Act of Parliament

usurper one who takes the throne without authority

vassal a person or country under the control of or in a dependent position to another

INDEX

A
American colonies 20, 21, 22, 29
Anne, Queen 30, 31
Aragon, Catherine of (queen of Henry VIII) 4, 5, 9
Armada 11, 12
Arthur, Prince of Wales 3
Authorised Bible 8

B
Babington Plot 12
Barebone's Parliament 26
Bible 9, 18, 19
Black Rod 23
Blenheim, battle of 31
Boleyn, Anne (queen of Henry VIII) 5
Book of Common Prayer 8, 9
Boscobel 25
Bosworth Field, battle of 2
Bothwell, Earl of 11, 13
Boyne, battle of the 31
Burbage, James 13
Burgundy, Margaret, Duchess of 2, 3

C
Cabot, John 14
Calais, loss of 10
Catesby, Robert 18
Catholics 8, 9, 11, 18, 26, 27, 29, 30, 31
Cavaliers 24, 25
Charles I, King 22-25
Charles II, King 16, 25, 26, 27-29
Church, separates from Rome 5
Churchill, John, Duke of Marlborough 31
Civil War 24-25
Clarendon Code 27
Cleves, Anne of (queen of Henry VIII) 5, 7
clothes
  Elizabethan 12
  Puritan 26
  Stuart 23
coffee houses 32
colonies, in America 19, 20-21, 22, 29
Columbus, Christopher 14
Commonwealth 26
court life 12-13
Cranmer, Thomas, Archbishop of Canterbury 4, 5, 8, 10
Cromwell, Oliver 24, 25, 26
Cromwell, Richard 27
Cromwell, Thomas 5, 7
currency 2, 3

D
Darnley, Lord 11, 13, 18
Declaration of Indulgence 29
De la Pole, Edward (White Rose of England) 3
divine right of kings 23
Drake, Sir Francis 12, 14, 15
Drogheda, Statute of (Poynings Law) 3
Dudley, Guildford 8
Dutch War 28-29

E
Edgehill, battle of 24
Edward VI, King 5, 6, 7, 8
Effingham, Lord Howard of 12
Elizabeth I, Queen 5, 7, 10-15
Elizabeth of York 2
Essex, Earl of 15
exclusion movement 29
explorers 8, 13, 14, 15, 19

F
Faerie Queene 13
Fairfax, General 25
Fawkes, Guy 18
Field of Cloth of Gold 5
Finch, Sir John 23
Flodden Field, battle of 5
France, war with 5
Frobisher, Martin 12
furniture, Stuart 23

G
galleons 14-15
George I, King 31
Globe Theatre 13
Glorious Revolution 30
Golden Hind 15
Great Britain, birth of 32
Great Fire of London 28, 29
Great Plague 27
Great Rebellion 24
Grey, Lady Jane 8-9
Gunpowder Plot 18

H
Hampton Court 10
Hanover, house of 31
Hardwick, Bess 10
Hawkins, John 12, 13
Henrietta Maria, Queen 21
Henry VII, King 2-3, 4, 14
Henry VIII, King 1, 3, 4-7, 9
Hepburn, James *see* Bothwell
Holbein, Hans 7
Holland, war with 26, 27, 28, 29
home rule, in Ireland 3
Howard, Catherine (queen of Henry VIII) 5, 6, 7, 10
Howard, Thomas, Earl of Surrey 5
Hudson Bay Company 20

I
Ireland 1, 3, 6-7, 15, 30, 31
Ironsides 25

J
James I, King of England, and James VI, King of Scotland 11, 12, 13, 15, 18-19, 22
James II, King 29-30
James IV of Scotland 5
judges 3
Julius II, Pope 5

K
Kildare, Lord 2

L
Latimer, Bishop 10
Lloyd, Edward 32
Lowestoft, battle of 29
Luther, Martin 8

M
madrigals 4, 13
Marlowe, Christopher 13
Marsden Moor, battle of 24, 25
Mary, Queen of Scots 11, 14
Mary I, Queen 5, 7, 8, 9-10
Mary II, Queen 29, 30
Mary Rose 6, 7, 14
Mayflower 20-21
Medway, battle of the 29
Middle Ages 1
monasteries 5-6
Monk, General George 29
Monmouth, Duke of (Protestant Duke) 29
More, Sir Thomas 4, 5, 7
Morley, Thomas 13
music 4, 13

N
Naseby, battle of 24, 25
naval powers 14
navigation equipment 15
New Model Army 24, 25
New Testament, in English 4
Northumberland, Duke of (Protector) 8

P
palaces, Tudor 10
Parliament, Acts of 5
Parliament 18, 22-26, 27, 32
Parliament in Ireland 3
Parliamentarians *see* Roundheads
Parr, Catherine (queen of Henry VIII) 6, 7
Pepys, Samuel 27, 28
Philip II, King of Spain 9, 12
Pilgrim Fathers 20
Pius V, Pope 13
playwrights 13
Pocahontas, princess 20
Poyning, Sir Edward 3
Presbyterians 24
printing press 3, 4
Protestant martyrs 10
Protestants 8, 9, 31
Puritans 19, 20, 22, 26, 27

R
Raleigh, Sir Walter 14, 15
Reformation 1, 4, 8, 9, 19
Renaissance 1, 4
Richard III, King 2
Ridley, Bishop 10

Rizzio, David 11, 13
Roman Catholics 8, 9, 18, 27, 29, 30
Roundheads 24
Royal Charles 28, 29
Royalists *see* Cavaliers
royal oak 25
Rump Parliament 26
Rupert, Prince 25
Ryswick, treaty of 31

S
Scotland
union with England 32
war with England 5
Sedgemoor, battle of 29
Settlement, Act of 30, 32
Settlers, early 20
Seymour, Jane (queen of Henry VIII) 5
Seymour, William 19
Shakespeare, William 13
Sidney, Sir Philip 12, 13
Simnel, Lambert 2-3
slaves 20, 29
Smith, Captain John 20
Somerset, Duke of (Protector) 6, 8
Spain, war with 12, 14
Spenser, Edmund 13
Spurs, battle of 5
Star Chamber, Court of 24
Stuart (*previously* Stewart), house of 17,1 9, 31
Stuart, James Francis Edward (the Old Pretender) 32
Stuart, Lady Arabella 19
Stuart, Mary *see* Mary Queen of Scots

T
taxes 22, 23
Thanksgiving Day 20
Theatre, Elizabethan 13
Tories 30
Tower of London 9
Triumphs of Oriana 13

U
Uniformity, Acts of 8, 9
Union, Acts of 6, 32
Union Jack flag 32

V
Van Dyck, Anton 22
Villiers, George 21

W
Wales, union with England 6
Warbeck, Perkin 3
Wars of the Roses 2
War of the Spanish Succession 31
Warwick, Edward, Earl of 2
Whigs 29, 30, 31
William III, King (William of Orange) 29, 30, 31
Williams, Roger 21
Wolsey, Thomas, Cardinal 3, 4
Wren, Sir Christopher 28
Wyatt, Sir Thomas 9

Y
York, Elizabeth of 2
York, house of 2
York, Richard, Duke of (Prince in the Tower) 3

ACKNOWLEDGMENTS

The publisher would like to thank the following for supplying additional illustrations for this book:

Picture research: Alex Goldberg, Elaine Willis

page 1, The Family of Henry VIII, The Royal Collection © Her Majesty The Queen; pp8-9, Edward VI's coronation, The Bridgeman Art Library; p10, Burning Bishops, The Mansell Collection; p10, Hampton Court, Mark Peppé; p11, Elizabeth I, The Bridgeman Art Library; p18, James I, The Bridgeman Art Library; p25, Charles II in oak tree, Mark Peppé; p27, the Great Plague, Mark Peppé